Caroline

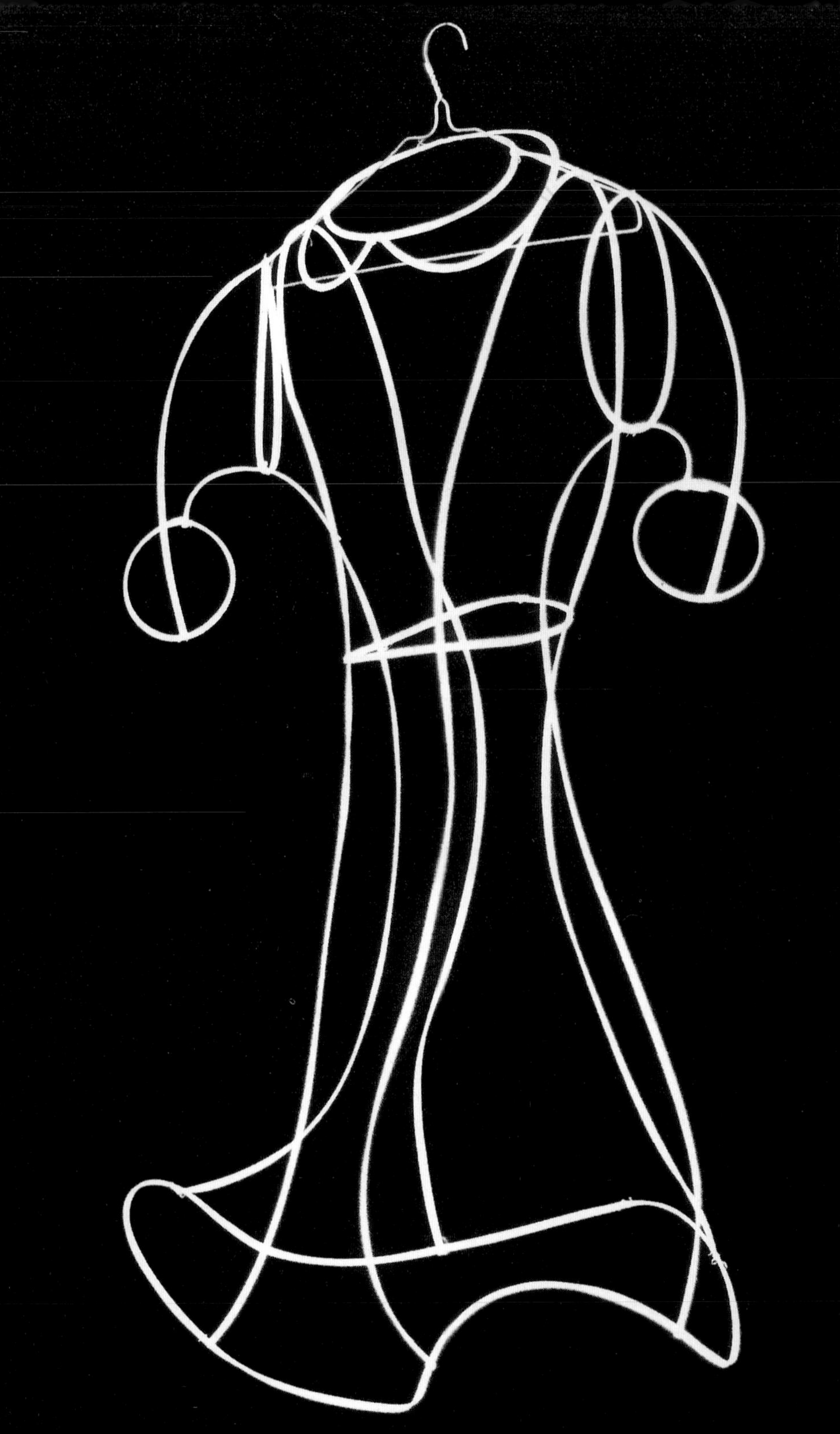

Caroline Broadhead

Jewellery in Studio

John Houston

Bellew Publishing CC

First published in Great Britain in 1990 by
Bellew Publishing Company Limited
7 Southampton Place, London WC1A 2DR

This book was funded by the Crafts Council

Designed by Ray Carpenter

British Library Cataloguing in Publication Data
Houston, John, *1935* –
Jewellery in studio: Caroline Broadhead. –
(Craft in studio).
1. English jewellery. Broadhead, Caroline
I. Title II. Series
739.27092

ISBN 0 947792 48 1

Overleaf. 'Underwear
outerwear' detail 2 1989
Cotton and nylon

Contents

'22 in 1' armpiece 1984
Cotton and nylon
(see page 45)

Introduction: *John Houston*

CAROLINE BROADHEAD began her career as a jeweller – a craft that in Europe has long been conventionally defined (and literally been given its value) by its use of precious materials. But since the 1970s she has progressively redefined her jewellery in terms of different values and more accessible qualities. Her artefacts formed a series of radical, reductive and sensuous proposals about the nature of ornament. They are a distinctive part of jewellery's *New Tradition* – an adventurous consensus of European talents that in two decades has evolved a formal language of ordinary materials, informal expression and multiple production. A modest language, but an ambitious project.

This has been the reinvention of the art (and craft) of jewellery as a recognizably late-twentieth-century form: a thoughtful synthesis of exotic and vernacular genres, Bauhaus theatre modes and modernist morality that takes the whole body as its site of action. This new practice, so often rigorously applied, was cheerfully humanized by Broadhead's graceful interventions in the early 1980s. Her veils and sleeves and shirts acquired a formal eloquence: they began to speak (but very gently) of fundamental states.

Ornaments speak to us about ourselves. But to what end: the revelation or the disguise of inner states? Ornaments *were* potent, precious; at first applied to sacred rites, then later privileged by secular power and wealth. But democracy has undone most of that. Once a sign of public reputation, such jewellery is now a private relic. In the late twentieth century the search has been for a personal authenticity of form and feeling.

Her earlier artefacts – from soft-look ivory to flexible woven nylon-strand objects – had a broad appeal, even beyond the fringes of the craft world, into areas of design and fashion. The fashion connection continues through C&N, the button and jewellery product company that Nuala Jamison and she formed in 1978. That certainly is design-based; their objects are predictable, planned products. Those buttons and other ornaments were fashion accessories, added elements within a 'classic' mode of women's clothing: Jean Muir was their first client, and the restrained, structurally inventive nature of her designs is what C&N hope for in their work.

But such design is shaped by practical economic constraints that do not apply to Broadhead's work as an individual jeweller. In fact it was the pressure to sell her work before she was ready to, before she had developed an idea to her own satisfaction, that formed her decision in 1978 to earn her living in other – though related – ways. Since then, teaching jewellery and working as a jobbing designer-jeweller through C&N have supported her other activities as a maker. One effect of this self-subsidy (she admits and regrets) has been to change the nature of that making (well, probably) by fishing it out of the stream of everyday motives and practices. Stranded on a dwindling island of available time, that work is more and more concerned with manifesting human relations, aspirations; as time shrinks, her objects – the clothing proposals – are becoming even more formally precise, linear, transparent. They are growing closer to drawings, silhouettes, with volume implied as *empty space.* Her silhouettes – the 'Seam' series, and now photographs of garments arranged to define the edges of a further *invisible* garment – are literally empty. Being fabric, these edges have a soft spring and curl, and a *hang,* which suggests a virtual weightlessness in relation to other types of sculpture (a category which is lightly brushed by Broadhead's artefacts). The fact that they do hang up-ends sculptural assumptions (clothes-hanger as weightless plinth?) and returns the 'Seam' garments to the realm of drawing – where they hover ambiguously among dress patterns, axonometric projections and cartoon images of animated (but *empty*) clothes. They are dynamic signs of a recent departure.

How do Broadhead's artefacts work? Looking back along her career as individual jeweller-maker-artist it is hardly possible not to see (and be powerfully impressed by) certain preoccupations with specific material and psychological modes. As she says: 'It's always possible to shuffle them all into a line, afterwards.' But what is most clearly evident as progress in techniques and images can also be detected in individual pieces of work, virtually from the start of her career in 1973. In that year she began the series of silver and ivory jewels in which the main feature is a curved piece of ivory that has been carved to represent a knotted strand of flexible material. The ivory's curve is continuous with the remaining part of the mainly silver neckband.

This series begins a sequence of work in which material and formal characteristics grow steadily more flexible and linear. The ivory, its nature softened by illusory carving, was soon to be visually dissolved in bangles which were decorated overall with strands of transparent colour. This threadlike painting led on to soft jewellery, composed of brilliantly coloured silk and cotton threads wrapped around cylinders, with bracelets and necklaces achieved with looser threads and tufts and tassels as articulation. The next steps – from thread to nylon tufts set in wooden frames, then into objects composed from a single strand of nylon – these confirmed the nature of her progress.

Her work has consistently proposed new hierarchies of materials and techniques; she has progressively softened, reduced and dissolved the constructive elements in her artefacts, replacing metal with ivory, ivory with thread and tassels, exchanging opaque thread for transparent tufts of nylon dyed in brilliant spurts of colour, discarding the tuft's wood bases and weaving her jewels entirely in translucent monofilament, dyed to evanescent, reflective sheens (increasingly like hair, like flesh, in the ways this new stuff holds the light).

The final small-scale artefacts (before the first enveloping garment of 1982-3) were already containers, but without a fixed form. Transparent, flexible, neutral (in terms of the conspicuous materials of hand-made jewellery) these woven nylon objects were also adjustable, their basic tubular structure capable of extension and retraction. Hovering on the borders of aesthetic self-sufficiency, these diaphanous carapaces were sturdy enough to stand alone, but also yielding enough to be worn gracefully. But, when worn, the most extendable of these pieces became transformed into visual metaphor. An arm-piece and a neck-piece could each be adjusted – into sleeve and veil. Both, but in particular the veil, create potent, ambiguous and disturbing images when worn. Some imagined union of the synthetic and the organic refers the viewer towards birth-cauls as well as veils, to tender membranes (protecting the wearer, yet themselves vulnerable), to cocoons and other more sinister web-spun bindings. These associations exist as faint but influential traces within a powerfully glamorous image. Indeed David Ward's photograph of the veil being worn (on the front cover of this book) has established this image as an icon within Broadhead's career so far. After this come garments concerned with their own structures through a process of altering, multiplying or exposing elements; by analogy, these visual commentaries speak for the absent, universal body whose states of feeling are incorporated in the modified garments.

Structural ambiguities attract meaning. The 'Seam' garments exist on several levels: as flexible drawings (shape without form), as transparent signs (clothing as idea), as overlapping layers (depth without measure). These references help to shape and question the image of these objects: the image remains potent *and* inconclusive while the garments represent a schematic memory of a person. But once they are placed on a living body that memory is erased, absence is replaced by presence, and the overlapping layers become a diagram of real space, existing in the real time of dressing and undressing. Caroline Broadhead puts on and takes off a range of these garments in 'Undercover' (the 1989 collaborative performance with Fran Cottell). The metaphor of transparency survives: as the layers of white outline are added to a real body (already completely clothed in black) there is a growing sense of intrusion and frustration; these garments betray the wearer – extra layers only measure an increased depth of illicit knowledge given, unwittingly, to the audience. Other images, overlapping interpretations, and a wish always to find meaning in such an allegorical performance tend to make such events into minefields of metaphor, with members of the audience (such as me) frequently hoist with their own petard.

The journey into metaphor has been a journey from substance into image. Broadhead's *practice* as a maker has been to find materials and techniques, and to make objects, which move towards greater degrees of transparency, flexibility and neutrality. By neutrality I mean that she chooses materials that are relatively value-free, unburdened with historical association, uninflected by social and aesthetic usages. Nylon monofilament has virtually no aesthetic pedigree; it traps light – the camera loves her tufted and woven artefacts – but it does not trap expectations. The woven nylon veil is an image dissolved by light. Her *practice,* consistently to dissolve whatever category, structure or image that she is working with (which is also the technical basis of cinematic montage), is a powerful psychological *process.* Each dissolution implies exposure – another image forming, another revelation melting into an overlapping sequence. The recent performances suggest that the single image is being dissolved into such montage sequences.

The latest extension of this practice takes the form of Broadhead's own photographs of clothing. These garments, shown as pale material on a dark background, are crumpled into a flowing ring of fabric. The centre of the ring is defined by the inner edge of these clothes tracing a dark empty shape on the background. The edge, a-flutter with the rumpled rhythm of the real clothing, defines a simple garment: short sleeves, round neck, a plain waisted tunic, ending at the hips. It's the costume equivalent of a classical torso (sans head, sans arms), but the main fact of its presence is that it is absent: a phantom product of the object-ground relationship. Its existence as a garment is only notional, in comparison with the inseparably defining fabrics (three real shirts). All these words to fix what is in fact (in perception) a fluctuating image: one of the classic optical ambiguities. Equally fast and fleeting, the social metaphors arise: absence and presence, substance and image; the formal deceptions of represenation. But in plain artefact terms, the image still connects with jewellery and beyond (just as jewellery is a fluctuating notion in the fictional world of ornament). Bracelet around wrist is substance around presence: inert artefact given its full human meaning when worn. Broadhead has arranged ordinary materials to portray sites of presence, states of absence.

Her earliest bangles and these latest photographic prints are equally images of what we mean (some of those meanings) when we clothe and ornament ourselves. In terms of her own development these prints are another step in the dissolving process that constitutes her practice. In literal terms, both substance and the central image have been dissolved. Her work continues to report on ornament's invisible domain.

Caroline Broadhead in her own words

This does include some questions from John Houston (JH in the text) about recent work and practice. The whole section is the edited result of two long tape-recorded conversations between these two.

Broadhead implies that the change in her work, from forms of jewellery to forms of clothing, has left jewellery behind. The change took place in 1982 and left her with all sorts of dilemmas which recent work continues to solve. There is a further implication, which is not really addressed here, that her recent work has carried her basic concerns beyond those of the modern crafts. We did not discuss it because her interests and her words are about work: the frame of theory is irrelevant to her unless it clarifies practice in specific ways.

However, I would like to propose a theoretical framework which might assist the reader of this book to consider jewellery and clothing in the same craft context. The crafts have transformed themselves during the twentieth century. A complex social and aesthetic evolution has changed some of the surviving crafts from a type *of production into a* mode *of practice. Although the post-industrial crafts were once a piecemeal nostalgia for older ways and means, the transformed crafts have become potentially vivid forms of enquiry: ways of questioning the nature of materials, testing the mind of the maker.*

In Britain especially, this mode has been developed to speak directly to an audience through a humanized sense of material and within domestic territory. Even when they are art as well as craft, these artefacts and events are rooted in common experience: their world is the familiar. Ornament, as here in Caroline Broadhead's career, can span this world, and find original forms to speak eloquently about inarticulate feeling.

"Henry's pelt was put on sundry walls
where it did much resemble Henry and
them persons was delighted.
Especially his long and glowing tail
by all them was admired, and visitors.
They whistled: This is it!"

John Berryman
From number 16 of
The Dream Songs (1964, 1968)

CB: . . . it was an opening-up for me that you could shape metal and colour metal and construct things with it. That was at Dartington. I was there for two years (1966–8); it wasn't taken as a class – it was just an area where you could go and work. It was supervised by a potter, Bernard Forrester, who had a very gentle and free way of thinking. So, if you wanted to enamel something you just held it in the flame of a Bunsen burner to do it. It was a straightforward, no-nonsense approach. I just made a few things there – they were very crude. I didn't see it as a career. Then I went off to Leicester to do foundation.

After Leicester there were three years doing jewellery at the Central [School of Art and Design, London]. There was Wendy [Ramshaw], Gijs Bakker and Emmy van Leersum. Apart from their presence as teachers it wasn't a terribly inspiring time – partly because I was such an awful student.

When I first made jewellery at Dartington, the sole purpose was wearing it. You made earrings and stuck them on your ears. That was the first thing that was exciting about it. However, almost simultaneously I was interested in what they looked like and what you could construct. Then there was this bit in the middle when I went to college. It should have been cancelled, really. Afterwards, I think that I picked up where I left off at Dartington. College had hypothetical situations where you made things for a client, who had lots of money, wanted gold and diamonds and a bit of individuality; and you were the little person who said, 'Oh, does that look nice to you?' I can't bear that. So that interlude at the Central was not my way of working at all.

After Art School

It was only after art school – when Nuala and Julia and I set up our Dryden Street workshop, fairly straight after – that I started making pieces that I liked. I suppose it was the freedom – nobody looking over your shoulder and about to comment, and the freedom from anybody else's expectations. There wasn't a word that you had to be, there wasn't this *artist-craftsman*, or the idea that the next step *is* . . . In fact, the next step then (1972–3), was that you got a job, or if you didn't live in London you went home and looked around from there. The idea of starting a workshop did seem terribly silly. It was very risky – people kept saying, 'How are you going to pay the rent?' It was like putting on a set of blinkers and saying we'll do it because we want to – and cross our fingers and see if we last. We didn't consider teaching because we were so much in the situation of learning things, and learning things on all fronts. Although most of us were using silver there was an awful lot to learn on the materials front – and on the business side, and on the survival side: how do you sell things and how do you go and get exhibitions? So I don't think any of us felt that we could teach anybody anything for quite a number of years.

JH: *I have a general memory of the jewellery field at that time in, and out of, the art schools, and the jewellers were certainly the most orderly and*

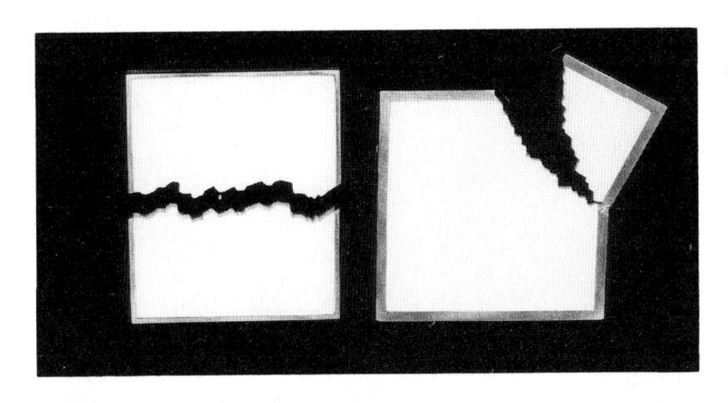

1. Brooches 1976
Silver and ivory

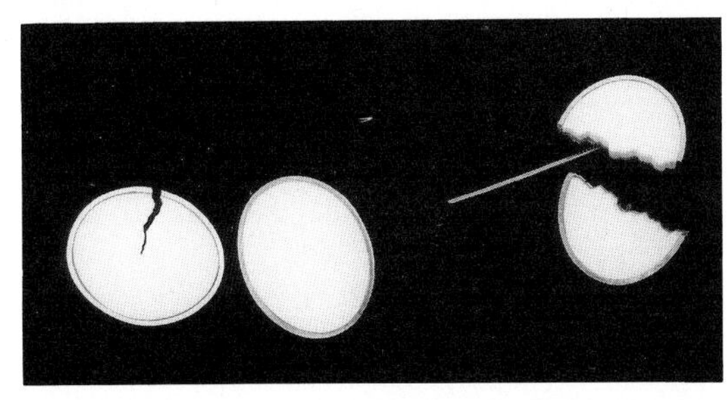

2. Earrings, pin and earring
1976 Silver and ivory

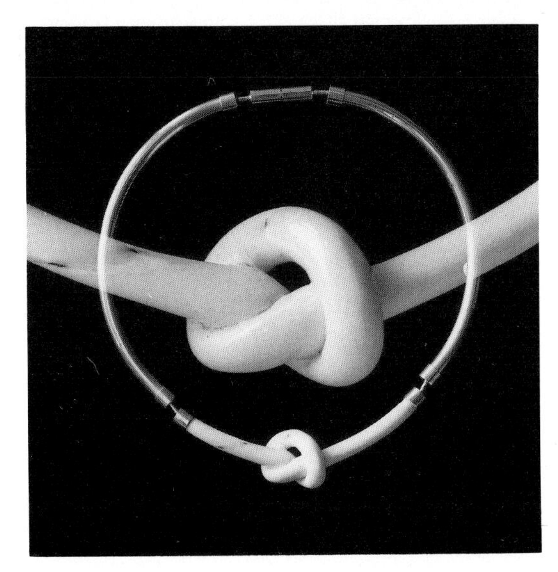

3. Necklace 1973
Silver and ivory

commercially aware group – the most committed to business, and to being businesslike in terms of designing and making their work. But Dryden Street had a very different quality. The place and the work, and the three of you as well, as far as the visitor could tell, seemed relaxed, informal, light-hearted and unconcerned about being a jewellery 'business'. Although none of you was being didactically avant-garde there was a credible difference of purpose in your work and the way you presented yourselves. I know that other people felt this just as clearly.

CB: I think, with hindsight, it was definitely something to do with not having any sense of business about it. We didn't do that consciously – we were there because we wanted to produce something, not to earn a living: that was a secondary thing. And I didn't earn a living from jewellery, not for five or six years. We all did the wedding-ring and the engagement-ring to make some money, and I got a part-time job selling books. There were all sorts of desperate struggles, financially – but we were very lucky to get somewhere that was so cheap. Sometimes we let a bit of the space to make some money. And it was just about cheap enough so that you could sell just one or two pieces in a month and still pay the rent.

Motive and Multiples

When I started making those knot necklaces [curved sections of ivory, carved to resemble a soft strip, that had been 'tied' in a knot] they were what I would like to wear. Friends bought some; that was exciting. Someone taking it away, someone you liked – that was someone really *in* my life.

That's why making multiples – repeating things to make them more accessible – was making things for people like oneself. It was more instinctive than pre-planned. The only things that we initiated were *Fourways* and the two *Two Day Shop* events. [*Fourways* was an exhibition of bangles and rings by Caroline Broadhead, Susanna Heron, Nuala Jamison and Julia Manheim. Each of them provided five bangles and five rings made as repeatable items: 'multiples' and 'limited editions'. Planned

4. Bracelet 1977
Coloured ivory

5. Bracelet 1977
Ivory and cotton

and organized by the makers, the show toured Britain and Holland between 1977 and 1978, visiting museums and specialist galleries. The materials used included silver, but always in combination with non-precious stuffs: ivory, mother-of-pearl, ebony, shell, perspex, resins and cotton. These makers opened their Covent Garden workshop to the public for *Two Day Shop* at the beginning of May in 1980 and 1981. The jewellers Ros Perry and Eric Spiller also took part, both times, and six Dutch jewellers were part of the second *Shop*.] C&N has taken over that side of things now. So I don't have to worry so much about saying 'I want to do it so I can wear it, or my friends can wear it.'

The work gets made in relation to feeling: nothing ever direct. It's more to do with knowing a sort of feeling I want from the pieces, and that's to do with the elements of simplicity, some sort of humour or wit, and something you can ponder upon: something that's an instant image and can also bear further looking at. That's not really a starting-point, but it's knowing what you want from something. That's a sort of aim. I never think in words about my work, so beyond those feelings I find it hard to put into words. However, there were three of us in the workshop so we were always talking and always criticizing our own and each other's work. That was a very big plus at that point; because whatever ups and downs you had there was always someone there to give support. And there was a feeling that you were discovering something every time you made a piece. It didn't look like anybody else's. We were always very watchful of what other jewellers were doing, but we didn't intellectualize about it; didn't put it into words. We were keen to watch their new work: you felt that you were on the front of something. It was very exciting. There was a degree of competition, even among the three of us, but it was a creative competitiveness – simply to do better.

6. Necklace 1976
Cotton

7. Bracelet 1977
Bound cotton

9. 'Loopy' necklace 1976
Bound cotton

8. Necklace 1979
Bound cotton

10. Necklace 1976
Bound cotton

11. Necklace 1977
Bound cotton

Materials

As to the materials I used, I moved from silver and ivory jewellery to cotton in about 1976 or 1977. I did a ring in ivory while I was still at College, but it was only when I was in Dryden Street that I made the knot necklaces. [Each was a single piece of ivory, carved to represent a flexible curved strip with a single central knot.] Some other ivory pieces were decorated with thin lines of colour: some people say that the move to coloured strands of cotton was the inevitable next step! But with all my work, if you arrange it out of its real sequence you can see coherent links! In fact, I've always proceeded by two steps forward, one step back.

The thread jewellery came about because I wanted to do something that was quicker than ivory, and already I wasn't happy about using it, and I wanted to use colour. I'd stopped myself using cotton for a very long time, because of what David Poston had done with it, and I didn't want to be seen to be copying him. Then I just decided that it was silly to have such an attitude and I would just try and see what happened. I also had the feeling at that time that I wanted to sell my work elsewhere, other than in jewellery galleries and through exhibitions. I wanted to have it alongside clothes, and the cotton seemed like the right material to sell with garments.

There were a few boutiques that had it. But they didn't understand that it had to be handled separately. In one shop – I think it was Howie's – they had them all heaped up in a rather scratchy basket. Although they weren't very expensive they still cost quite a lot for that kind of thing, and how on earth could they expect people to buy them when they were all scrunched up and getting dirty?

But almost simultaneously other people were asking for it – Galerie Ra in Amsterdam and others. They were very enthusaistic about it, which I hadn't expected at all because I'd been aiming the work somewhere else. And I was thinking, you can't have that – it's cotton! But then I saw that what I was doing with the cotton (all the tufts and wraps and colour) wasn't at all like David Poston's work. He had always woven in his ends,

12. Tufted necklace 1979
Tufted nylon, veneered wood and silver casing

13. Tufted belt necklace and bracelet 1979 & 1978
Tufted nylon, veneered wood and silver casing

14/15. Two brooches 1979
Metal and nylon

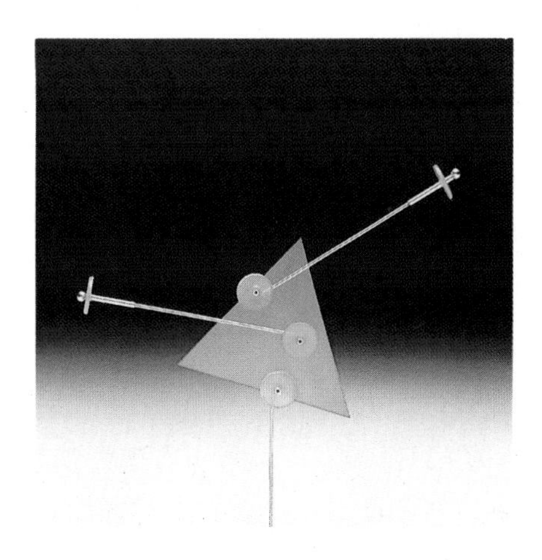

and wrapped them up tightly and securely so that nobody would ever see them. Whereas I realized that the tufts and so on were the best bit for me. Once I had grasped that I didn't mind about the connection.

JH: *The cotton jewellery now seems the beginning of a fundamental change in the way you worked and, possibly, an equally important change in the way you thought about jewellery. As you've said, cotton thread made it possible for you to work much faster – a silver and ivory necklace could take one, even two weeks to complete, but you could make five cotton necklaces in a day, two in an evening. There were other advantages too: a freedom to modify work as it was being made, changing colour and proportions quite spontaneously; and the chance for ideas to evolve more quickly. This is also the period (1977–8) when you spent five months in Africa and, coincidentally, made some more decisions about how you wanted to work.*

CB: The African trip was an amazing experience, an adventure: mainly because it was real travel by road, gradual and difficult, not flying. So it was camp-sites, not airports; real local markets, not supermarkets. It was close to people's lives and a test, for us, to see how you communicate: how you can assess people when none of the normal clues of dress and language are there; all the things and signs that you rely on without realizing that you do. In a different culture, on a different continent, none of those things can be grasped so readily.

The Decision

I did make a big decision, on coming back from Africa, that I didn't want to have to make a living from my jewellery any more. I had thought that the time in Africa would be separate from my work, but I surprised myself. I kept doing little drawings of how I could solve problems in my work at that time. Until then I had felt that I might still change to some other activity, but this was the moment when I knew that jewellery was what I really wanted to do. So it was by being denied the workshop that

16. Flexible bracelets and push-on brooches 1981 Nylon line and sheet

some sort of decision was being made. I wanted to pursue my ideas fully – not to sell them immediately when they were only a month old. That's when the tufted thing became my work. I'd been playing around with nylon-tufting before I went to Africa, but done nothing I liked. I'd made a single piece with tufts – the wood had split and everything had gone wrong with it. But having had this break I started planning straight away. I got a teaching job at Brighton Polytechnic and Nuala and I started C&N at that point – in 1978.

[C&N developed from plastic jewellery and buttons made by Nuala Jamison for the fashion designer Jean Muir. Caroline and Nuala generally collaborate on design and production. A sub-contractor cuts up their basic shapes; they do all the subsequent cutting, polishing, dyeing and fixing.

17. Expanding bracelet and push-together bracelet 1982 Nylon line, tufted nylon and boxwood

18. Push-together bracelet 1980 Tufted nylon and laminated wood

All the work is to order, for shops and fashion shows in Britain and the USA. Most of it is simple and restrained: subservient to the fashion garments although not attempting to be 'fashion' jewellery.]

At first the tufted jewellery was made in hoops – embroidery hoops. I covered the circular hoops in silver and then I decided that the metal was superfluous and that I would make my own veneers. Since I couldn't make circular frames I began to work on different shapes.

Skill

I've never really considered myself a craftsperson. I've always struggled with making things. I've never felt I was good enough at making: I always see the rough edges that shouldn't be there. In fact the first time I did the cotton, which didn't involve much skill – although it does involve some – I knew I could manage. 'The next time,' I said to myself, 'I'm going to make something that I *can* make well.'

So my way in to the woven nylon things was saying, 'Now I definitely don't want to have technical problems here: I don't want to find that the nylon scratches, or the wood splits when you pull tufts through it, or the silver splits down the solder seam,' all the problems I had been having. The nylon line was a nice material that I could colour and it didn't need anything else – so there was nothing else to have a problem with.

I never have a clear image of what I'm about to do. In fact if anything that's about the only thing that's hard and fast: that I actually like being lost, having to find something. It's like a blank sheet of paper that's got to be filled and you've got no idea of what to do.

Development

JH: *But just as you're choosing your material, your nylon strand, and feeling comfortable about it – do you find yourself saying, 'I want to say* this, *and I know how to say it'. Or is it just a vague evolution, with you happy in your choice of material? Is there always a material base which enables you to work, because you are unworried about the stuff, and about the technique?*

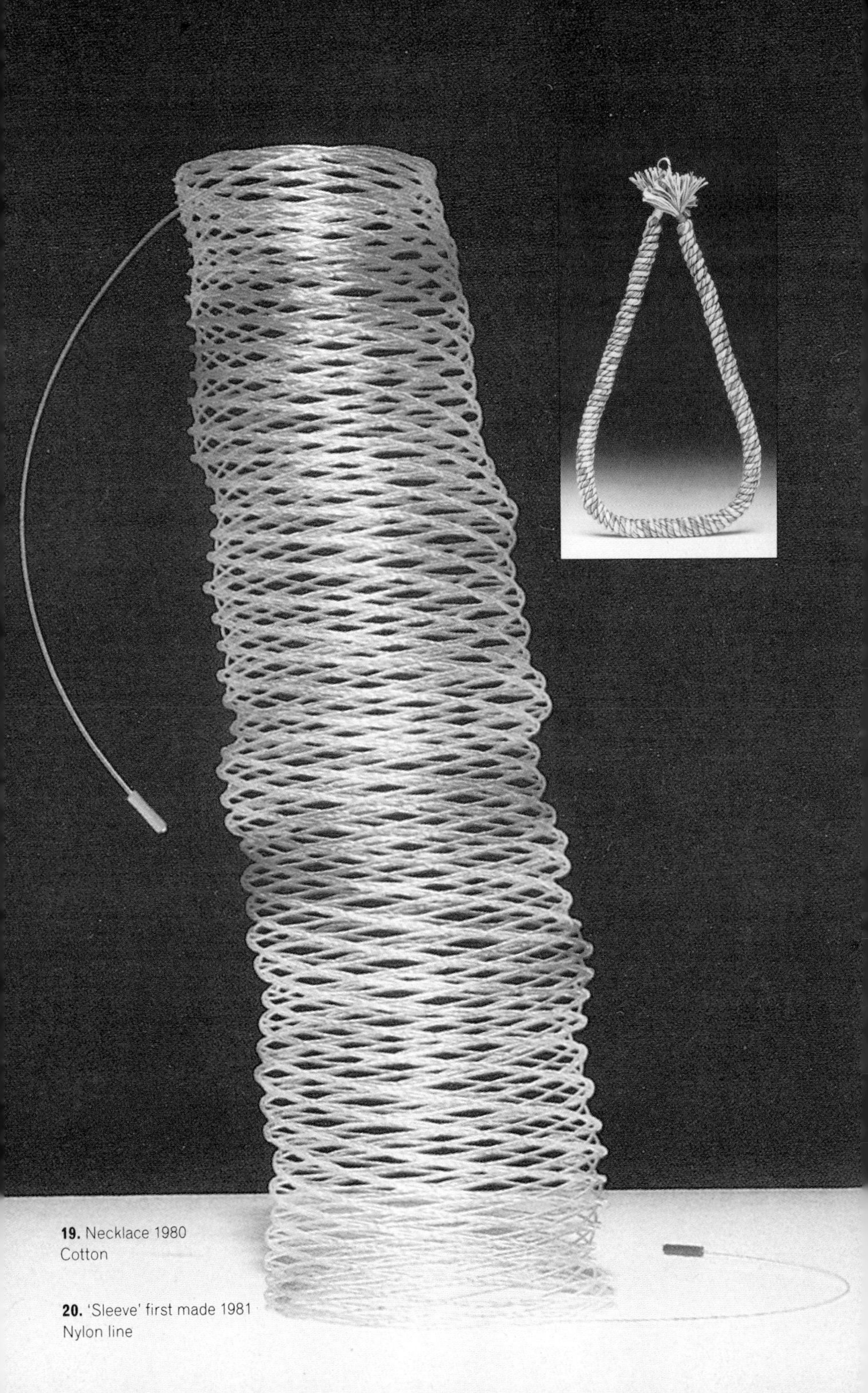

19. Necklace 1980
Cotton

20. 'Sleeve' first made 1981
Nylon line

21. Woven necklace and
sphere bracelet 1981
Nylon line

23. Woven necklace and
sphere bracelet 1981
Nylon line

22. Bracelet 1981
Nylon line

CB: I'm not sure . . . when I first did a woven piece I didn't like it. I was going to throw it out. But then it probably was Nuala who said, 'That's quite nice' and I said, 'No, no, it's all too regular.' But having been encouraged to keep thinking about it, I did it all again and discovered it had all these peculiar qualities. But I had been wanting something much more ethereal, much more hazy. I didn't like its repeated structure, looking like knitting. But as it happened – and I didn't really make it do that – this structure had a flexibility and range of adjustment that did suit me well. It was a happy accident. But in a way, even though it sounds a bit pretentious, I let the work do what it wants to do.

JH: *Let your work do the talking?*

CB: No, let it do the *walking*! Because in the end the work does decide: it develops itself. There is an idea – which has several branches you can pursue. But then you stop the train of thought and say, 'Very well, I'll pursue them'; then the work, while you are doing it, has a life of its own. You can make it go, but only where it wants to.

The Dutch Connection

I went to Amsterdam [in 1982 on the proceeds of a Crafts Council Bursary] because I felt there was an awful lot going on. I thought it would be good to be based there – I knew quite a lot of people because of exhibition contacts. It had become the Paris or New York of the jewellery world, as London had been during Electrum's heyday. Now it was Galerie Ra acting as a focus and there were jewellers coming out of the woodwork all over the city!

JH: *The Dutch avant-garde had already ambushed jewellery and tried to strip it of its face value as commodity capital. They had been very successful in reconstituting it as a series of genres that were defined by the body. In the case of Emmy van Leersum and Gijs Bakker the whole naked body became jewellery's prime site. An egalitarian and rational approach prevailed during the late 1960s and early 1970s and established ways of working and thinking that were scrupulous, refined and increasingly self-referential. Their impulse – to dramatize and define the body – was realized in serious and generous ways; thereafter, both problems and solutions seemed merely ingenious for a while.*

There were parallels to all this in Britain, with David Poston (and you, later on in the 1970s) choosing a non-precious material, such as thread, and making semi-private jewels: objects giving pleasure to the wearer; but outside the hierarchy of status signs. So this simplicity had a humanizing role – but not programmatic like the Dutch. Much of their good jewellery retained a sense of social drama, but rather dogmatic: 'Behave like this, be frank, be open, be honest – like this bracelet, it's rubber and aluminium.' But your jewellery doesn't have this narrative element. In fact, I hardly dare say it – your jewels are like flowers.

CB: Hold it! That's just what the Dutch said they were. When Galerie Ra opened, it *was* all aluminium and rubber – serious, punchy stuff. When they had the British work over for the first time, apparently they were really cross and said, 'How could you have this folksy rubbish in the gallery?' That was my work, and they were outraged. All that colour, and it was soft, and far too feminine, and conspicuously handmade. It had all been enjoyed rather too much. Their regime demanded base metal or other ideologically OK materials. My stuff was the exact opposite. I think *Fourways* [touring exhibition of multiples jewellery made by Caroline Broadhead, Susanna Heron, Nuala Jamison and Julia Manheim; they also organized the show's tour of Britain and Holland] was the second British exhibition that got to Amsterdam, probably in 1978. (Galerie Ra opened in 1976.) That was when the outburst happened. Paul [Derrez – the jeweller-founder of the gallery] told me about it several years later. If he'd told me at the time I think I would have taken it a little more to heart.

What seems to have happened is that this input of pleasure-seeking work made such an impact on the Dutch that they began to do it themselves. All sorts of textile workers suddenly thought that jewellery

24. Tufted necklace 1979
Tufted nylon, veneered wood
and silver casing

25. Tufted necklace 1981
Tufted nylon and wood

was the right place to be. It did actually calm them down from being so righteous. So when I went out there in 1982 there was a lot of work being done in that way. But the last pieces that I'd done were the woven veil and the woven sleeve – so I was looking for pieces that went further than that. There were quite a lot of body-scale pieces around at the time.

Clothing

I'd always liked the earlier Dutch body-pieces – the 1970 'clothing suggestions' of Bakker and van Leersum, for instance – but my next step was more of an accident, and more an extension of what I was already doing. I didn't really mean to make a shirt. My woven pieces were the connection: you can turn them up – literally extend or retract the basic cylindrical form in a twisting, spiral movement. What excited me was this quality of expansion and contraction and the idea of a bracelet coming all the way up the arm. So the pieces that I did in Amsterdam were the long-sleeved shirts and that pale pink piece that goes round the neck, and then you tighten it. I had an exhibition at Galerie Ra. I offered the shirts – I knew I was treading on terribly tricky ground – but Paul Derrez didn't mind. He accepted the work right away. Still, when I came back to England I really didn't know if the shirts were a mistake or not.

There was a feeling from that exhibition that I had actually gone over the boundary. I was now doing clothes – so what was I going to do? It was a very difficult category. It wasn't going to be fashion: no question of producing things for each 'season'. And yet it wasn't jewellery, and there wasn't this thing called 'Art Clothing' or whatever my things are. I saw it in exactly the same way as I had all the other things, and yet it was a different thing. For a few years after that I did show pieces in jewellery exhibitions but they were wrong. It seemed like cheating people who'd gone to see jewellery and here was a garment. It didn't seem like the right place for it. So, in a way, I faded a bit at that time – I couldn't see quite where to put it. Still don't!

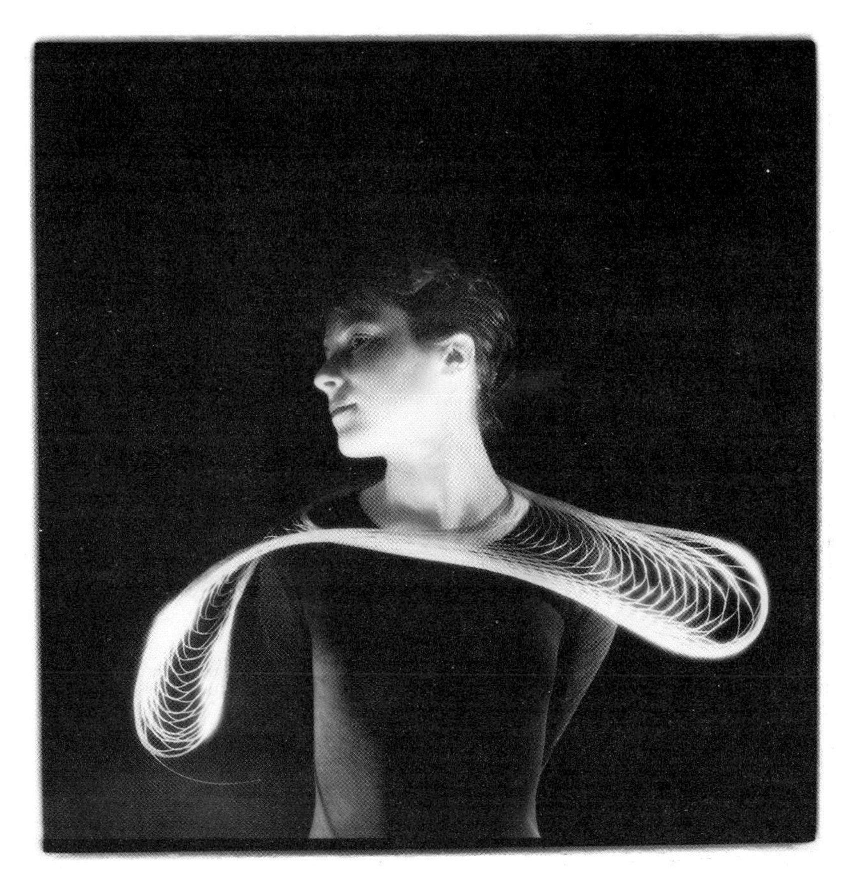

26. 'Stretch' woven necklace
1982 Nylon line

27. 'Small wrap-around shirt'
1983 Cotton

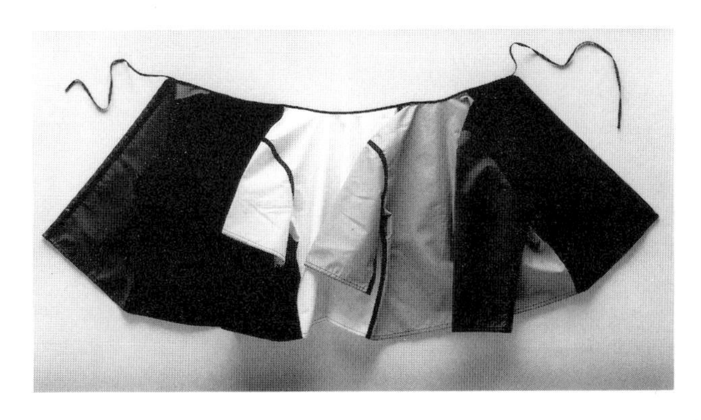

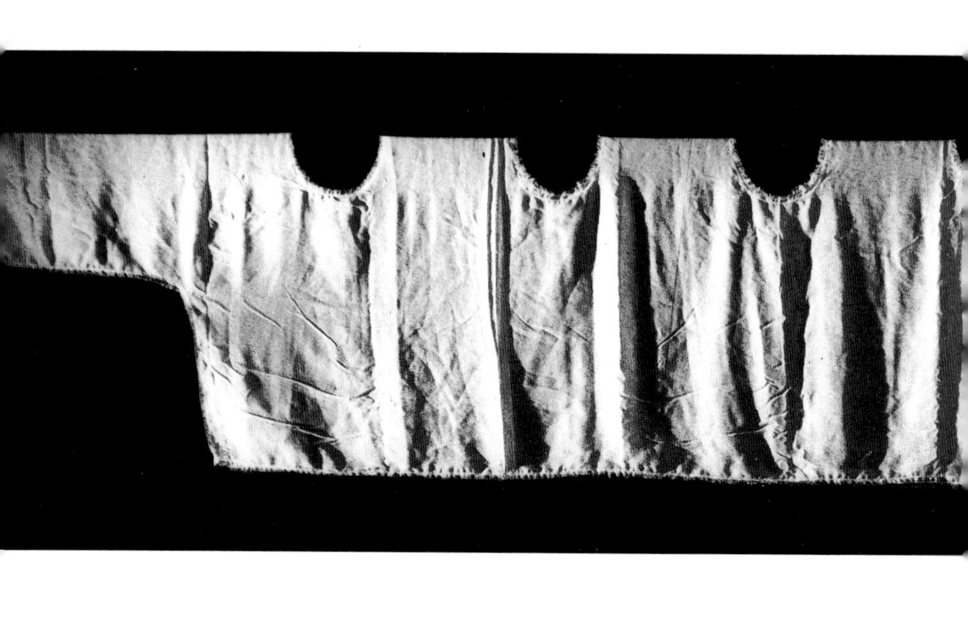

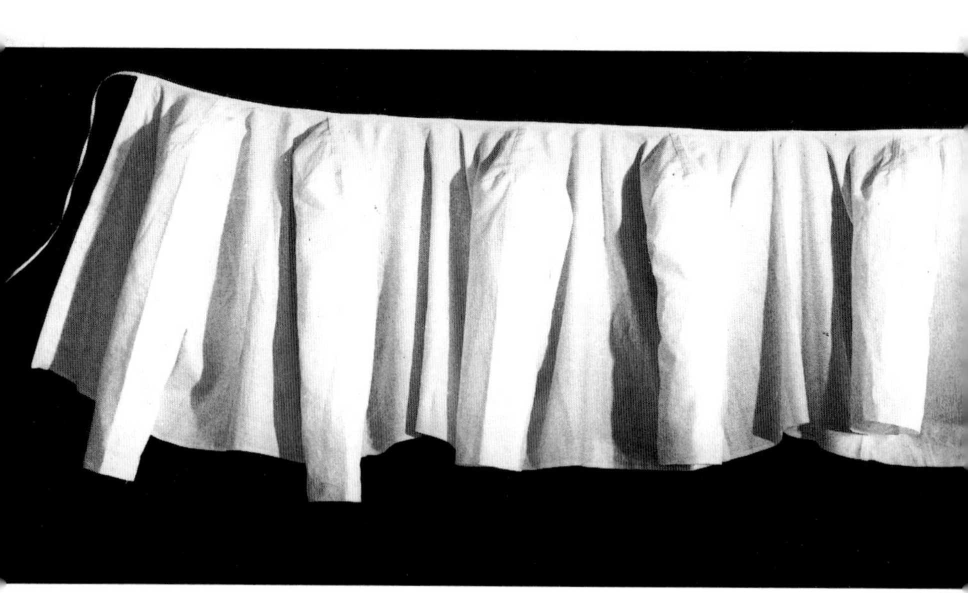

28. 'Fold up shirt with 7 necks'
1983 Silk georgette

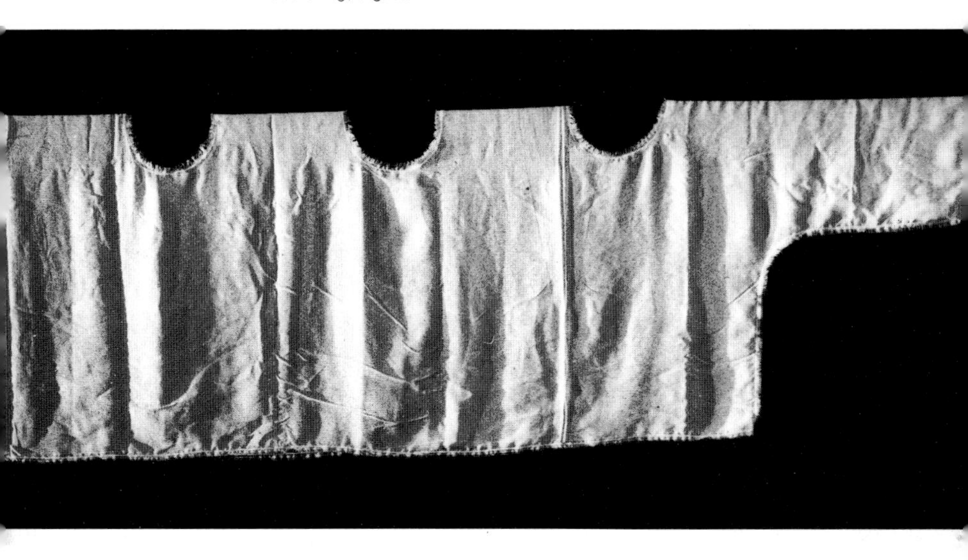

29. 'Round and round' shirt 1983 Cotton

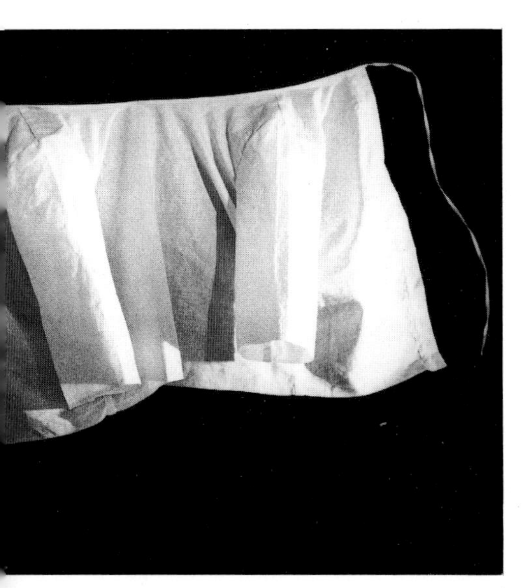

30. 'Shirt with long sleeves' 1982 Nylon

Conceptual Clothing 1986

JH: *I didn't see the 'Conceptual Clothing' show, but it sounded as though it was* exactly *the right place for you to be. It came at a time when you've said that you were feeling uncertain about your work, you thought that some of your wearables didn't really work in the context of jewellery exhibitions, where the audience had different expectations. Then after two years of doubt, this exhibition offered a space that was free from all those preconceptions about jewellery. But you didn't need that freedom. Your work had arrived precisely* at *the title.*

CB: I thought that my work fitted the title more than that of anybody else in the show. It was perfect for me. Some other work that might have fitted was missing for various reasons, and that made a difference to the look and meaning of what remained. It was a difficult show to shape successfully. But that's the same problem we all have, trying to find a form.

['Conceptual Clothing' was devised by Fran Cottell and Marian Schoettle and first shown at the Ikon Gallery in Birmingham at the end of 1986. It toured other sites in England and Scotland until early in 1988. It contained work by twenty-three artists, including Caroline Broadhead. The catalogue is a thoughtful introduction to work which is still resistant to the language of art criticism, perhaps because the works' own familiar social languages are still saturated with meanings that we assume but seldom speak. Despite this resistance, Broadhead's catalogue statement is useful:

> I am using the characteristic scale, proportions and features of garments and the familiarity of these to make clothing forms that express movements, aspirations, dilemmas, states and so on. Clothing holds a visual memory of the person and it is this closeness to the human being that I am interested in.

Judith Duffey's review in *Crafts* (No. 88 Sept/Oct 1987) sums up:

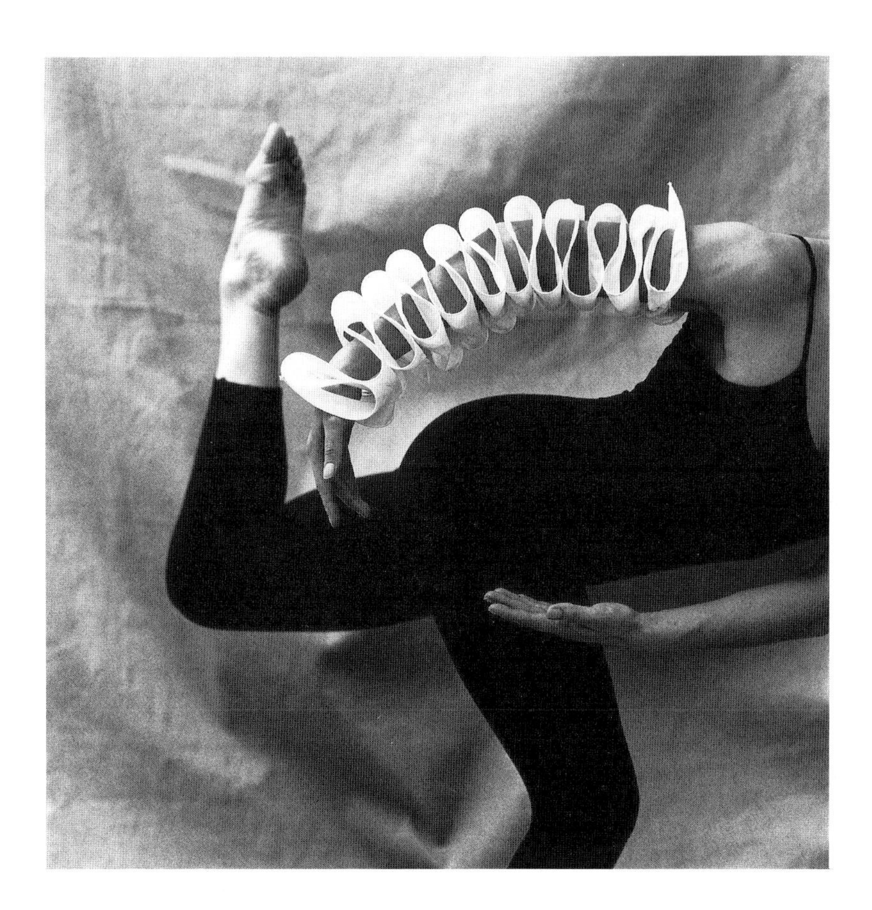

31. '22 in 1' armpiece 1984
Cotton and nylon

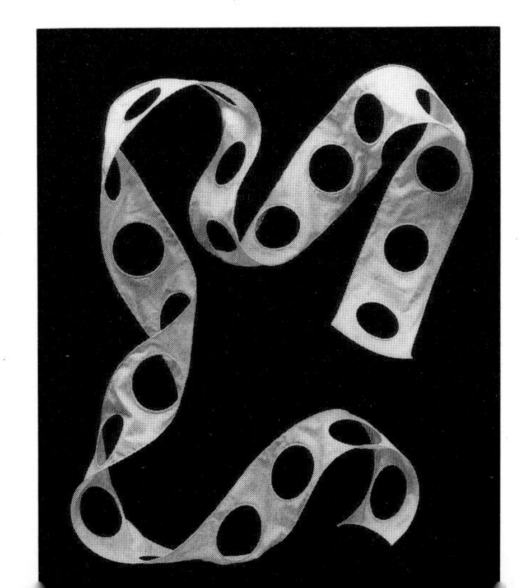

32. '22 in 1' armpiece 1984
Cotton and nylon

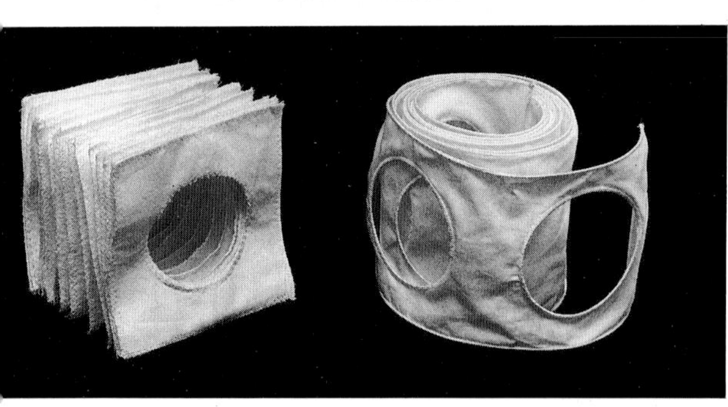

33. '18 Cushions' armpiece
1984 Cotton

34. '18 Cushions' and '22 in 1'
armpieces 1984
Cotton and nylon

35. 'Twin shirt' 1984
Silk

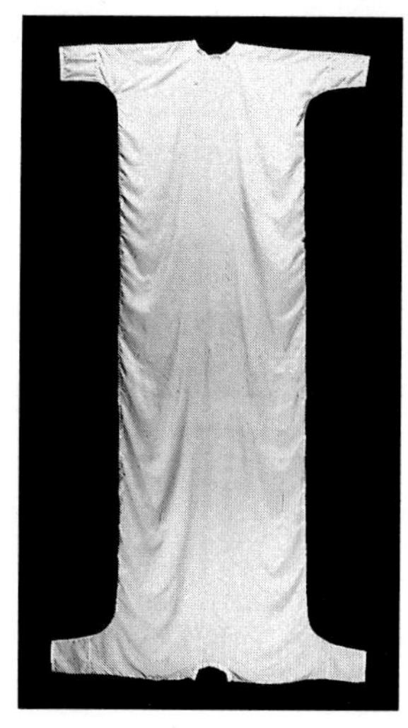

36. 'Twin shirt' 1984
Silk

Most successful in its sensitive fusion of technique and message was Caroline Broadhead's installation 'Seven Ages'. Traditional garment construction methods joined carefully different white fabrics to form metaphors for growth. Named stages – 'Cocoon, Stretch, Curling Up, Crumple' – describe simultaneously quality, form and process. In these, the doubly-sleeved 'Uniform, Carrying Other' (three progressively smaller shirts seamed into a continuous garment) and the ghostlike 'Seam', where substance disappeared and only the connecting process remained, the sewing techniques reinforced senses of entrapped regimentation, dependent responsibility and final dissolution.]

37. '7 ages: 1 Cocoon' 1986
Silk and nylon

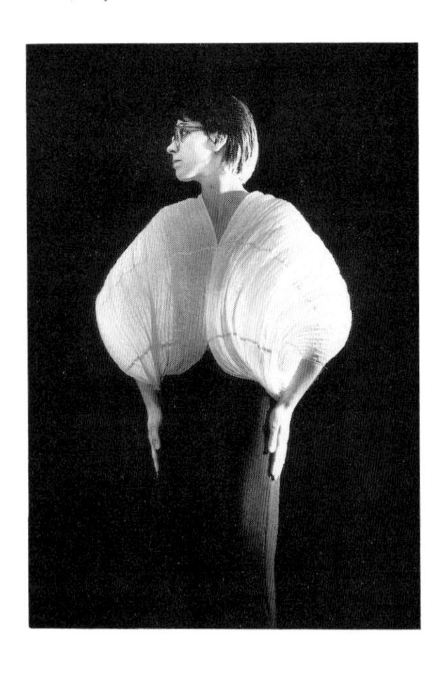

38/39. '7 ages: 1 Cocoon' 1986
Silk and nylon

Before 'Conceptual Clothing' it was a matter of 'the work takes up so much time – and so does teaching – and so do the kids'. So unless there's something very definite that's demanding work, it's very easy to let it slide and put your energies into something else. So when this show was planned I did work very hard. It was the perfect exhibition – so much about my kind of work. I only knew about some of the other people involved. But it was good having work in an art gallery – exciting *not* to be put in a showcase. And marvellous to be told 'that wall is yours' and being able to spread things out. What I did was in seven parts: I'd never seen it altogether before, so the big area was important to me.

My interest in the clothing is because of its closeness to the human being, but without being a portrait or a study or anything literal. For example, number six in the 'Seven Ages': it's called 'Crumple'. It was just really wanting to do something that wasn't ironed – wasn't as people expected a piece of clothing to be seen. In reality things are often crumpled and worn. It was trying to display something that wouldn't normally be on display. That's why the pins are there as well; it's part of the making and so not normally seen. It's an embarrasment – unacceptable. That was old age – fairly obvious. And number seven was 'Seam', the totally vacant garment. That's really been the last major piece I've done – the whole of the 'Seven Ages'.

40. '7 ages: 3 Uniform' 1986
Cotton

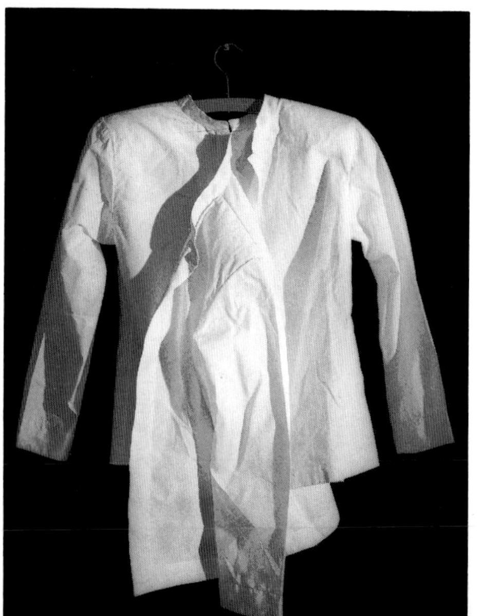

41. '7 ages: 6 Crumple' 1986
Linen and pins

42. '7 ages: 2 Stretch' 1986 Lace

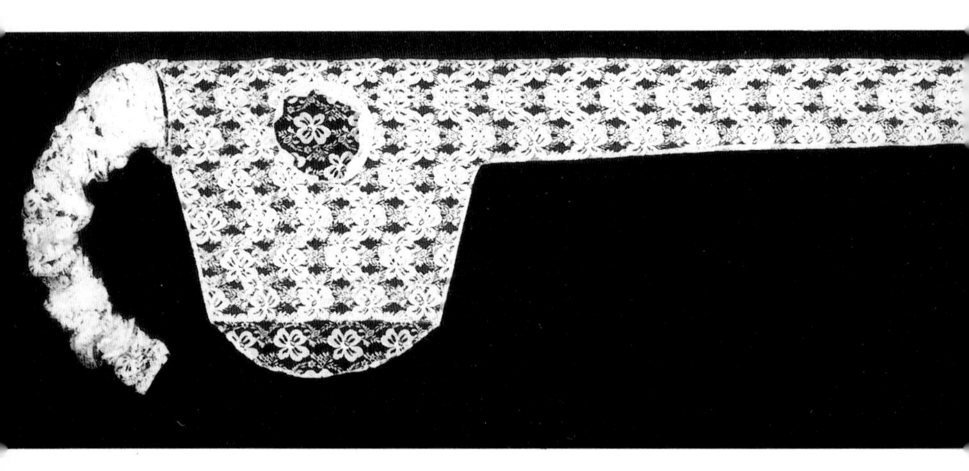

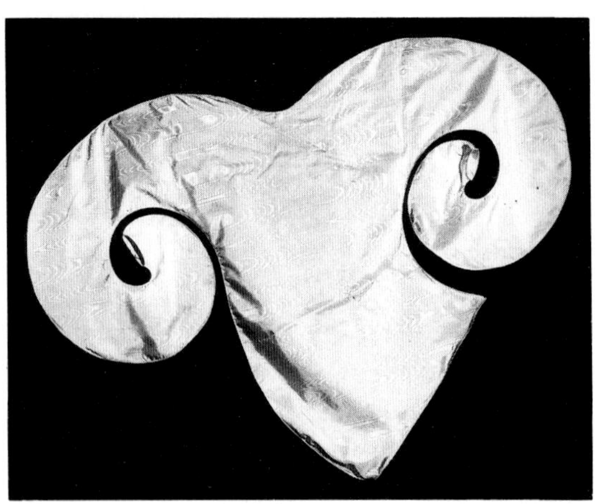

43. '7 ages: 4 Curling up' 1986 Moiré nylon

44. '7 ages: 5 Carrying people' 1986 Wool, nylon and viyella

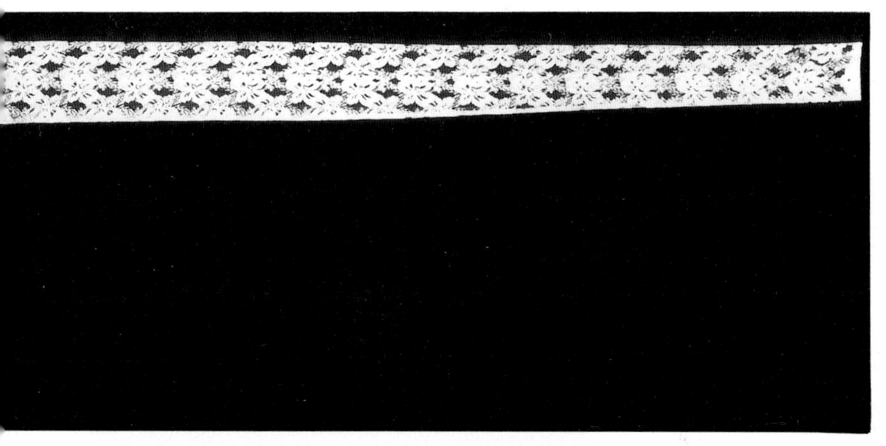

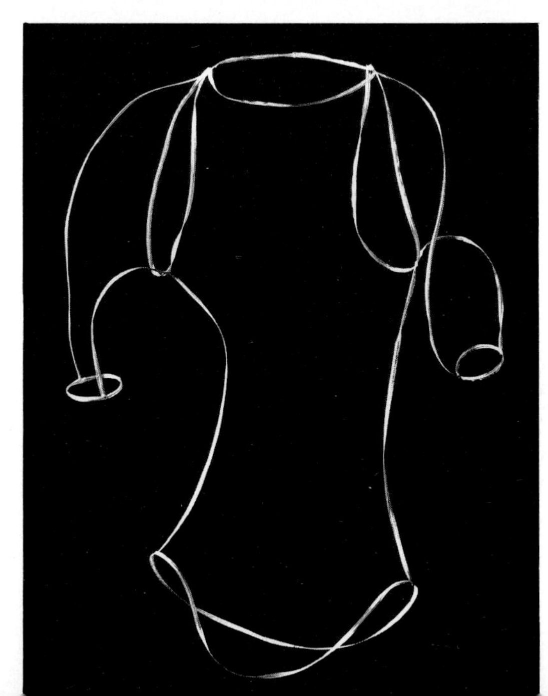

45. '7 ages: 7 Seam' 1986 Cotton and nylon

JH: *You seem to have got a progression in your work in which everything gets more and more like people.* Not *just because you have moved from artefacts to garments, and now use garments to make performances and photographs, but also because of changes in the actual* substance *of it. You have moved from silver and ivory to cotton, then to wood and nylon: the nylon-filament woven pieces assumed garment-like forms; then shirts, shifts, tunics that began to grow supra-human forms and to represent feeling in terms of the social nature of fabric, costume, basic elements of clothing; correspondences.*

CB: Yes, it all gets softer and softer.

JH: *Yes, and more fleshlike, too: at least up to the time of the armpiece and the veil which are fleshlike in their texture, pliability and the way they absorb and reflect light: their mix of opacity and translucency. The object has an ambiguous presence – is it ornament, garment or flesh? It's all three, but so inseparably dissolved in each other that the borders of each category are blurred. The decision poured from one category to another begins to melt the observer's assumptions.*

CB: That's interesting, I don't think I've seen it like that before. I carved ivory so that it looked soft – from the beginning.

JH: *Yes, I've only just realized that. When I first saw those pieces in the 1970s I thought they worked in a designy way – you've certainly got design qualities in your work.*

CB: Yes, there are elements of design, but not in that problem-solving way. I hate that approach: I've certainly noticed that shift – making things look soft, then making them in softer material, then making objects that were soft in themselves. I hadn't seen it as a progression, but I think it is.

'Undercover' Performance 1989

JH: *Now, the more recent 'Conceptual Clothing US/UK' event – the performance titled 'Undercover' that you and Fran Cottell put on at the end of 1989 at the Institute of Contemporary Arts, here in London, and in Philadelphia. Is this going to be a form you can continue working in for a time, or are you already beginning to resolve that?*

46. 'Undercover' performance (with Fran Cottell) London and Philadelphia 1989

CB: I don't know. I enjoyed doing it. However, just in terms of energy and time it was extraordinarily costly. To do a twenty-minute performance took weeks and weeks of preparation: making things, making slides, taping noises and so on. Neither of us have any equipment, we had to borrow cameras, borrow tape-recorders, borrow projectors to have a look at our slides. It's an uphill struggle. I thought it was exciting, but I don't think I'd ever want to do it on my own. I wouldn't have the courage on my own. I don't know whether Fran and I will develop along the same way, or whether somebody else would join with me . . .

One starts off with a little idea which is very easy to throw about, and then suddenly, all the practical things you need – sound, light and all the visual qualities – make it very complicated. Then it's no longer a simple thing to be played with. Instead it's complex layers of things that have to be connected to each other.

Everything gets more condensed. That's the difference between how I work now, and the way I worked in the early 1970s and later. What I do now is much more reliant on what's inside, than in looking for new materials or doing drawings to start ideas.

It's much more to do with the state of the personality. It's my personality in a way, but really I'm the keyhole. I'm not using a narrative and saying 'this is me'; it's more of a general state. I've made several pieces called 'Stretch'. Everybody knows what it's like to be stretched. It's a recognizable state, even though it comes from my experience.

JH: *Then there is the question of language. Not words, although your work sets plenty of problems for words such as jewellery, ornament, craft; even the word artefact is beginning to dissolve. As the prime concerns in your work move away from substance and towards allegory, those concerns have got wider and wider, even though we have been talking about greater detail appearing in your work.*

CB: But they are the same thing. Because you are closing in and expanding the detail. It's like looking at something tiny under a microscope. It becomes a huge image, and you can see all the detail.

JH: *Yes, even the smallest gesture can have a major function . . . You can see where the conversation is going. Unless you dissolve this new way of working, which there are signs that you're beginning to do . . .*

CB: Then I'm gone as well!

JH: *In a way, yes. What's happening now: what's the process and the practice? Have you stopped making things?*

CB: Oh no, but as always, work goes one step forward, then two steps back. It's never one line, although you can shuffle it all into a single line later on. But there are always several possibilities, so where's the certainty until you've finished a particular stage? I suppose that these photographs may still be in the middle of something themselves. They are actually a run-on from those skeleton garments [such as 'Seam' the x-ray tunic from the 1986 'Seven Ages'] in so far as the interest is the negative space formed by some surrounding garments. How is a person defined? How do you define the edges of a person? In this case, maybe it's other people, or what you wear. It's becoming ambiguous as to how you are made up.

There are other ones to do, where I want to have layers of things on one photograph – made by superimposing two different negatives on the same print. The layers will actually be floating on top of each other, a simultaneous image related to all the layers I was making in the performance.

47. 'Stretch' 1988 Cotton

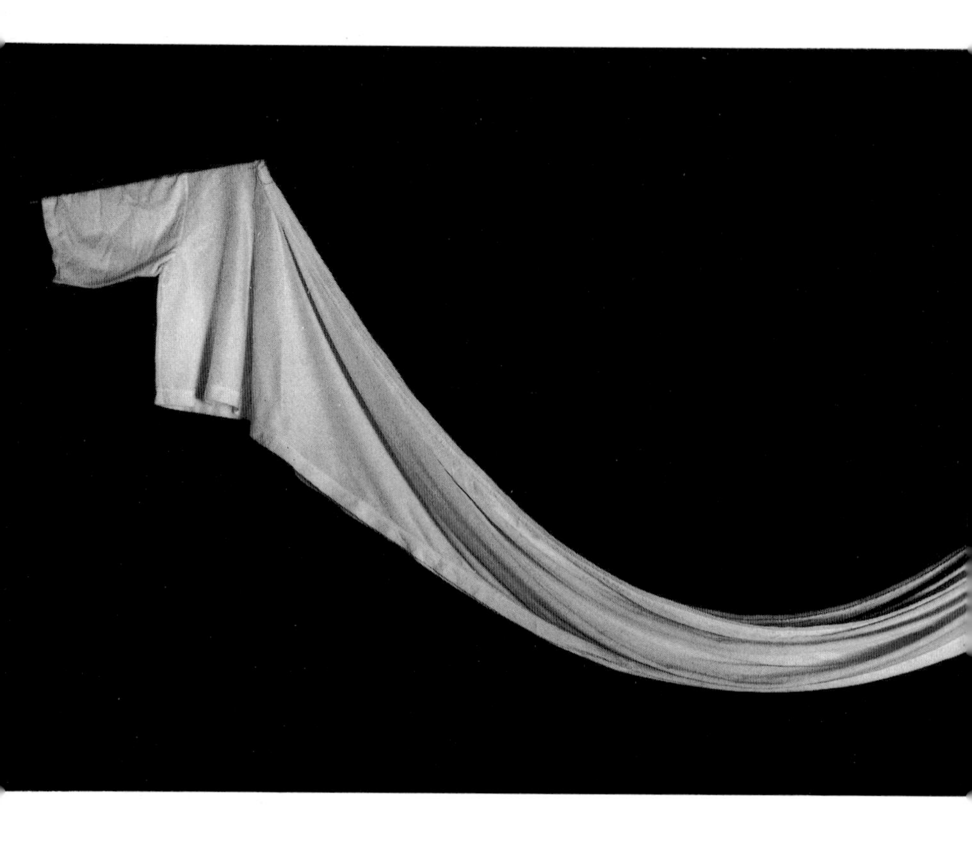

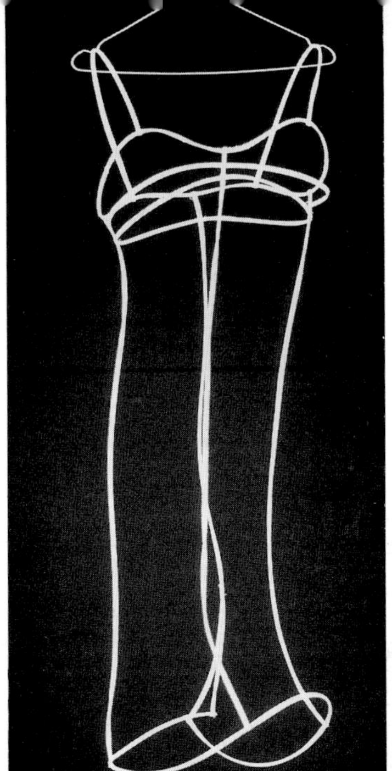

48. 'Underwear outerwear' detail 1 1989
Cotton and nylon

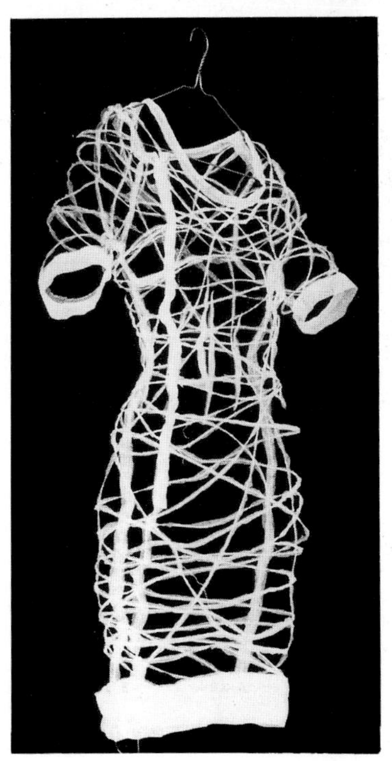

49. 'Web' 1989
Fabric and nylon

50. 'Invisible people' 1989
Photographic work

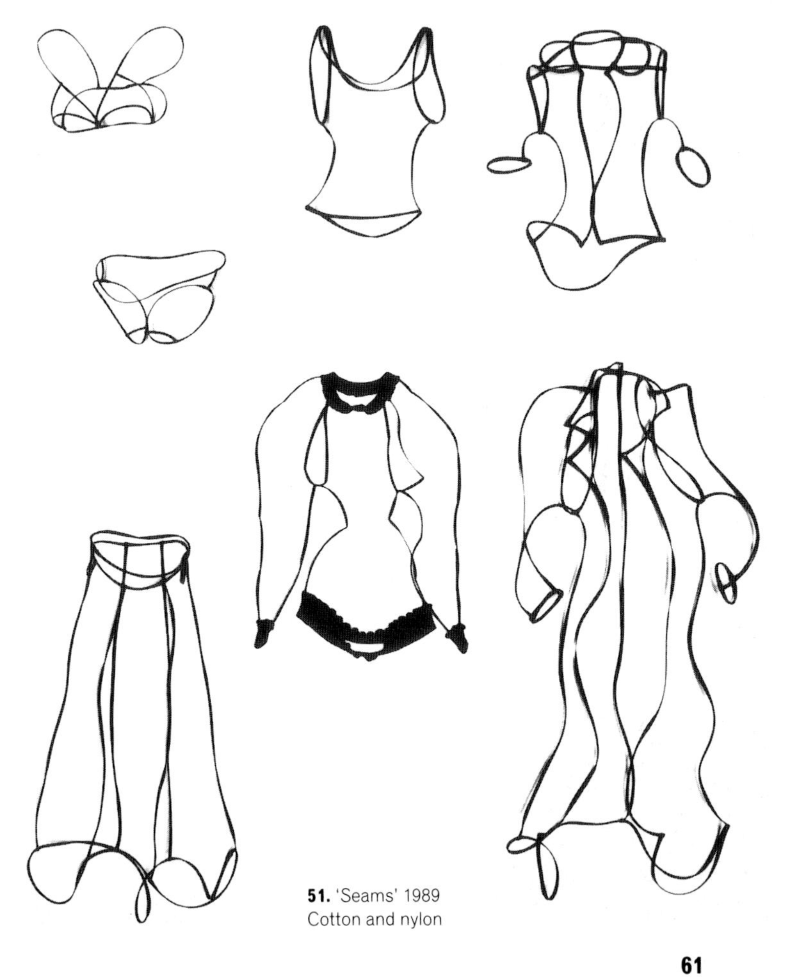

51. 'Seams' 1989
Cotton and nylon

Caroline Broadhead

1950 Born Leeds, West Yorkshire

Training

1968–9 Leicester School of Art
1969–72 Central School of Art & Design, London

Awards

1982 Crafts Council Bursary

Teaching

1978–87 Brighton Polytechnic
1987 to present Middlesex Polytechnic, London
1978 Five months driving from London to Kenya
1978 to present C&N Buttons & Jewellery Production in partnership with Nuala Jamison

Exhibitions

1976 **On Tour,** British Council/Crafts Council, touring West Germany and Australia
Six Jewellers, Midland Group, Nottingham
1977–9 **Fourways,** with Susanna Heron, Nuala Jamison, Julia Manheim, touring UK and Netherlands
1978–9 **British Jewellers on tour in Holland,** the Municipal Van Reekumgallery of Modern Art, Apeldoorn and tour of Netherlands
1979 **Caroline Broadhead Jewellery, Michael Brennand-Wood Thread Collages,** Crafts Advisory Committee, London
1980 **Caroline Broadhead,** solo exhibition, the Municipal Van Reekumgallery of Modern Art, Apeldoorn and tour of Netherlands
Two Day Shop, Dryden Street Gallery, London
Schmuck International 1900–1980, Kunstlerhaus, Vienna, Austria
Six British Artists, Art Latitude Gallery, New York, USA
1981 **Caroline Broadhead,** solo exhibition, Arnolfini, Bristol
Caroline Broadhead and Eric Spiller, Crafts Council Shop, Victoria & Albert Museum, London
Two Day Shop, Dryden Street Gallery, London
1982 **Caroline Broadhead,** solo exhibition, Galerie V & V, Vienna, Austria
Caroline Broadhead, solo exhibition, Galerie Ra, Amsterdam, Netherlands
Jewellery Redefined, British Crafts Centre, London
Views on Jewellery 1965–82, Stedelijk Museum, Amsterdam, Netherlands
1983 **Caroline Broadhead & Betty Woodman,** Galerie Het Kapelhuis, Amersfoort, Netherlands
New Departures in British Jewellery, American Craft Museum, New York, USA
The Jewellery Project, Crafts Council Gallery, London
1984 **Caroline Broadhead & Susanna Heron,** Cada Galerie, Munich, West Germany
Cross Currents, Powerhouse Museum, Sydney, Australia
Contemporary Jewellery, Museum of Modern Art, Kyoto, Japan
Whitechapel Open, London
1985 **Bodyworks & Wearable Sculpture,** Visual Arts Center, Alaska, USA
Whitechapel Open, London
New Tradition, British Crafts Centre, London

1986 **Caroline Broadhead – Recent Work,** solo exhibition, Norwich Castle Museum, Norfolk
Draagbaar, Kruithuis, s'Hertogenbosch, Netherlands
Asahi Craft Fair, Tokyo, Japan
British Design, Kunstlerhaus, Vienna, Austria
Whitechapel Open, London
Conceptual Clothing, Ikon Gallery, Birmingham and tour

1988 **Contemporary British Crafts,** Crafts Council/British Council Museums of Modern Art in Tokyo and Kyoto, Japan
Diversions on a Theme, with Jim Partridge, Martin Smith, Contemporary Applied Arts, London

1989 **Conceptual Clothing,** performance 'Undercover' with Fran Cottell, Institute of Contemporary Arts, London
Conceptual Clothing US/UK, performance 'Undercover' with Fran Cottell, Painted Bride Center, Philadelphia Pa, USA

1990 **Three Ways of Seeing:** Fred Baier, furniture; Caroline Broadhead, jewellery; Richard Slee, pottery, Crafts Council, London and tour

Publications

1974 **Tickling the Ivories,** Jacquey Visick, *Design* February

1976 **On Tour,** catalogue, British Council/Crafts Advisory Committee, London

1977 **Fourways,** leaflet

1978 **Fourways +,** *Arnolfini Review* July/August
British Jewellers on tour in Holland, the Municipal Van Reekumgallery of Modern Art, Apeldoorn, Netherlands

1979 **Ruffs & Cuffs,** *Crafts* No. 37 March/April

1980 **Caroline Broadhead,** catalogue, the Municipal Van Reekumgallery of Modern Art, Apeldoorn, Netherlands
Schmuck International 1900–1980, catalogue, Kunstlerhaus, Vienna, Austria

1981 **Caroline Broadhead,** catalogue, Arnolfini, Bristol
Soft Geometry, Paul Derrez, *Crafts* No. 53 November/December

1982 **Caroline Broadhead,** catalogue, Galerie Ra, Amsterdam, Netherlands
Jewellery Redefined, catalogue, British Crafts Centre, London

1983 **The Jewellery Project,** catalogue, Crafts Council, London
New Departures in British Jewellery, catalogue, Crafts Council, London
Caroline Broadhead & Betty Woodman, leaflet, Galerie het Kapelhuis, Amersfoort, Netherlands
Jewellery Undefined, Susanna Heron, *Crafts* No. 61 March/April

1984 **Jewellery International,** catalogue, American Crafts Museum, New York, USA
Contemporary Jewellery, catalogue, Kyoto Museum of Modern Art, Japan
Cross Currents, catalogue, Powerhouse Museum, Sydney, Australia

1985 **New Tradition,** catalogue, Caroline Broadhead, British Crafts Centre, London
Bodyworks & Wearable Sculpture, catalogue, Visual Arts Center, Alaska, USA
The New Jewellery, Peter Dormer & Ralph Turner, Thames & Hudson

1986 **Conceptual Clothing,** catalogue, Ikon Gallery, Birmingham

Caroline Broadhead, Gloria Dale, *Ornament* Spring

1987 **Conceptual Clothing,** Reviews, Judith Duffey, *Crafts* No. 88 September/October

1988 **Diversions on a Theme,** catalogue, Alison Britton, Contemporary Applied Arts, London

Contemporary British Crafts, catalogue, Crafts Council/British Council, Museums of Modern Art in Tokyo and Kyoto, Japan

The Art of Dressing, Judith Watt, *Guardian* 25 January

1989 **Conceptual Clothing US/UK,** catalogue, Painted Bride Art Center, Philadelphia Pa, USA

Collections

1976 Worshipful Company of Goldsmiths, London, *ivory and silver bracelets*

1977–83 Crafts Council, London, *ivory, cotton, nylon tufted and nylon woven pieces of jewellery*

1979 Shipley Art Gallery, Gateshead, *nylon tufted necklace, bracelet and earring*

1980 Gemeentelijke Van Reekumgallery, Apeldoorn, Netherlands, *cotton pieces*

1981 Israel Museum, Jerusalem

Castle Museum, Norwich, *woven piece*

1982 North West Arts Association, Manchester, *brooch*

1982–3 Stedelijk Museum, Amsterdam, Netherlands, *woven pieces*

1983 Kostum Museum, Den Haag, Netherlands

County Museum, Middlesbrough, Cleveland

Contemporary Art Society, gift to Bristol City Art Gallery, *woven bracelet*

1984 Crafts Board of the Australia Council, Sydney, Australia, *seven fabric pieces including two shirts*

Museum of Modern Art, Kyoto, Japan

The works illustrated are from private collections and the following:

Caroline Broadhead
Crafts Council
Lady Dale
Mrs A. Emgeg
John Jesse
National Museum of Modern Art Kyoto
Shipley Art Gallery

Photographic Credits

(references are to caption numbers)

Caroline Broadhead 48-50
Ray Carpenter 3
David Cripps 9, 10, 12, 13, 24, 25, 41, 47, 51
David Deary 46
Ian Dobbie 4
Nuala Jamison half-title page
Peter Mackertich 1, 2, 5-7, 11, 14-19, 21-23
Annie Morad 46
Graham Portlock 8
Dominic Richards 46
Charles Thomson 20
David Ward 20, 26-40, 42-45

The first verse of John Berryman's poem, number 16 of *The Dream Songs* (1964, 1968) is reprinted by permission of Faber and Faber Ltd, London.